The Gallery
would like to thank
IBM United Kingdom Limited
for financing the re-design
of this catalogue

Cover:
John Everett Millais: 1829–1896
Isabella

Simone Martini: **Christ Discovered in the Temple** (see page 16)

A Guide
to Pictures in
the Walker Art Gallery
Liverpool

Merseyside County Council
1980

Foreword

This illustrated guide to some of the finest and the most popular paintings in the Walker Art Gallery was first published in 1974 to celebrate the first hundred years of our achievement. It has now been revised and several more pictures added.

The foundation stone of the Gallery was laid on 28 September 1874 by Prince Alfred, Duke of Edinburgh and the building was opened by the Earl of Derby on 6 September 1877. It was the culmination of many years of planning and made possible ultimately by the generosity of Alderman Andrew Barclay Walker who paid for its building and after whom it is named.

Many paintings of many different schools and periods have entered the collection in this hundred years and more and the Gallery has also brought outstanding exhibitions of paintings to the public of Merseyside.

This guide gives a general introduction to the history of the Gallery and a commentary on the paintings illustrated which I hope the visitor may find useful and thought provoking. It is intended to complement the scholarly catalogues already published and in train on the whole collection, and as a souvenir as the Gallery enters its second century.

COUNCILLOR JOHN LAST
Chairman,
Arts and Culture Committee

Ercole de' Roberti: **Pietà** (see page 18)

The pictures in the Walker Art Gallery come from a variety of sources by gift, bequest and purchase, over a long term of years. Some are recent acquisitions, others date from the foundation of the Gallery itself in 1877, but by far the most precious, and chiefly the earliest pictures in date, have been in Liverpool since the end of the eighteenth century, in the collection of William Roscoe, the self-educated lawyer, philanthropist, banker, writer and collector. The Simone Martini and Ercole de' Roberti, illustrated on pages ii and 6, once belonged to him.

He is one of the most interesting characters in the history of Liverpool, and particularly for us, in the field of art. He was connected with the earliest societies of artists here which held exhibitions in the late eighteenth century; he knew and corresponded with artists and men of letters of the day; he wrote the first biography in English on Lorenzo de' Medici, the Florentine banker, whose enlightened patronage he attempted to emulate. He explained the purpose of his own collection for the advertisement in his sale catalogue of 1816:

> The following works have been collected during a series of years, chiefly for the purpose of illustrating, by a reference to original and authentic sources, the rise and progress of the arts in modern times, as well in Germany and Flanders as in Italy. They are, therefore not wholly to be judged of by their positive merits, but by a reference to the age in which they were produced. Their value chiefly depends on their authenticity, and the light they throw on the history of the arts.

From this sale, which was caused by Roscoe's financial difficulties, part of the collection finally passed to the Liverpool Royal Institution, which he had helped found. After long exhibition there it, was transferred on loan to the new Walker Art Gallery at the end of the nineteenth century. It was presented to the Gallery in 1948.

The Walker Art Gallery was founded initially to house the annual Autumn Exhibitions, organized since 1871 by Liverpool Corporation at the Museum, and which superseded the annual exhibitions of Liverpool Academy of Arts held since Roscoe's day. The building was presented by Alderman Andrew Barclay Walker and opened in 1877. The Gallery in its early years as well as organizing the Autumn Exhibition began forming a permanent collection and tried to buy both 'popular' and 'high art'. These dual objectives are underlined in the report on the first decade of the Gallery's activities:

> While endeavouring to secure works of the highest technical skill, the fact has not been lost sight of that the public, for whose education and instruction the institution in a great measure exists, delight in subjects of popular character and with this in view pictures have from time to time been added which by appealing to common feelings and sentiments of our daily life have afforded a fine moral lesson and great pleasure to the numerous visitors to the Gallery who are uninitiated in the higher forms of art.

This policy proved extremely successful and profits from the Liverpool Autumn Exhibitions gave the Gallery ample funds for purchasing such works as Yeames' *And When Did You Last See Your Father?* (p. 60) and Holiday's *Dante and Beatrice.* The early attendance figures have not been surpassed. In 1881 for instance, 610,799 people visited the gallery in 260 days. Most of the committee's purchasing was done from these exhibitions. This was seen as an incentive to leading artists of the day to send in. In the early years the Gallery kept abreast of new trends. Avant garde movements such as the Newlyn School and social realism were easily embraced: in 1882 *A Street in Brittany,* by the leader of the Newlyn School, Stanhope Forbes, was bought (p. 64). However, the sudden growth of the New English Art Club and the Camden Town Group outside the Royal Academy and largely outside the Liverpool Autumn Exhibitions made both the Gallery's exhibitions and the policy of buying from them less and less rewarding. From about 1910–12 the popularity of the Gallery and the success of the Autumn Exhibitions began seriously to decline. This decline meant that purchase funds diminished and acquisitions were far less ambitious than they had been in the days when Holman Hunt's *Triumph of the Innocents* had been acquired for £3,516. The impact of Roger Fry and Impressionism made the Gallery's permanent collection seem a ghastly mistake. However, moves were soon made to rectify the situation and to revitalize the Gallery. With the aid of generous bequests and gifts, five galleries were added and the entrance hall remodelled in 1931–2. From 1929 Liverpool Corporation had provided an annual picture purchase fund of £750. This remodelling and extension stimulated a debate on what should be the function and correct acquisitions policy of the Walker Art Gallery. Many wanted to see the Gallery build up a historical collection of British art from Tudor times. In 1932 Lord Wavertree, son of Sir Andrew Barclay Walker, died and bequeathed £20,000 in addition to his collection of silver and pictures. This promptly provided the Gallery with the wherewithall to follow a policy such as that pressed for by Councillor Rathbone, Colonel Cotton and others, of acquiring British paintings of all periods. From 1933 acquisitions were made following this new programme and works like Wilson's calm and majestic *Snowdon from Llyn Nantlle* (p. 44) and Gilman's *Mrs Mounter* (p. 74) were acquired.

In 1945 the Gallery received the important Emma Holt Bequest, one of the most important ever donated. This is the only surviving collection of the many formed by Liverpool merchants in the nineteenth century and remains in the house of its collector, George Holt, Emma Holt's father. Formed essentially of nineteenth century British paintings it includes outstanding works by Turner (p. 14), Gainsborough (p. 90) and Bonington.

Since the 1950s the emphasis has been on enlarging foreign representation, with works by Rembrandt, Ruysdael, Rubens and Murillo. By a combination of funds from the rates, donations from Liverpool firms and individuals and from other sources such as the National Art Collections Fund and government grants administered through the Victoria and Albert Museum it has been possible to acquire an impressive group of paintings by the French Impressionists and subsequent schools – Degas, Cézanne, Seurat and others. At the same time the collection of contemporary British art has continued to grow, and aspects of local art, both contemporary and historical, are receiving increasing attention.

Complementing the permanent collection is the broad programme of exhibitions covering all aspects of painting and related subjects organized by the Gallery. Most important of these are the John Moores Liverpool Exhibition and the Peter Moores Liverpool Project. The first brings a panorama of new British paintings to Merseyside, the second focuses in depth on a narrow field of contemporary British or European art. This outstanding patronage, unparalleled elsewhere, enables Merseyside to see and enjoy something of the very varied and lively art of today. John and Peter Moores have generously presented many of the notable pictures from these exhibitions. A new departure is in the field of photography which is taking on a renewed significance as an art form.

Many strands therefore make up Merseyside's collection and it continues to expand in the furtherance of the Gallery's aim to represent the best in European art of all periods.

William Hogarth: **David Garrick as Richard III**
(see page 39)

Some Events
in the Gallery's History

1850   Association of citizens formed to promote the establishment of an Art Gallery, Library and Museum. Negotiations with the Liverpool Royal Institution to take over their collection came to nothing.

1852   *Atalanta and Meleager* by Charles le Brun (1619–1690), Liverpool's first important Old Master, presented to the Corporation by Mr Benjamin. Act of Parliament to allow establishment of a public library, museum and art gallery.

1871   First Liverpool Autumn Exhibition organized by the Corporation on the lines of the Royal Academy's annual exhibition, held at the museum. Admission charges one shilling, six pence, and three pence.

1873   Alderman Andrew Barclay Walker offered to present a Gallery to Liverpool to commemorate his term as Mayor.

1874   28 September: Prince Alfred, Duke of Edinburgh laid the foundation stone of the Walker Art Gallery, built to the designs of Cornelius Sherlock and H.H.Vale of Liverpool and named after the donor. £1,200 was set aside by the Council for the purchase of works of art.

1877   6 September: the Walker Art Gallery opened by the 15th Earl of Derby. 324,117 visitors in four months.

1878   *And When Did You Last See Your Father?* by W.F.Yeames bought from the Liverpool Autumn Exhibition for £750 and just under £3,000 spent on purchases.

1881   610,779 visitors, an unsurpassed attendance.

1881–91   Three paintings by Pre-Raphaelites purchased to commemorate Liverpool Academy's association with the Pre-Raphaelite Brotherhood in the 1850s. 1881: *Dante's Dream* by D.G. Rossetti, £1,575. 1884: *Isabella* by Millais, £1,050. 1891: *Triumph of the Innocents* by Holman Hunt, £3,516 (of which £2,016 by subscription).

1882–86   Paintings by the social realists bought: *A Street in Brittany* by Stanhope Forbes. 1886: *Hard Times* by Fred Brown.

1884   New Extension opened. Paid for by Sir Andrew Barclay Walker.

1886   Grand Loan Exhibition of pictures, first large loan exhibition mostly of 19th century artists.

Exhibition
in the Gallery
1888

1891   *Punishment of Luxury* by Giovanni Segantini (1858–1899), bought for £315, one of the few modern foreign pictures bought before 1900.

1893   Large part of the Liverpool Royal Institution collection deposited. Bequest of £2,000 by the 15th Earl of Derby. The income from it to be used for purchase of paintings to encourage rising artists.

1896   *Sponsa de Libano* by Edward Burne-Jones bought for £750.

1904   404,419 visitors.

1908   Historical Exhibition of Liverpool Art, a comprehensive show covering the eighteenth and nineteenth century, marking the beginning of serious study and collecting of local art and patronage.

1910   *Horse Frightened by a Lion* by George Stubbs, born in Liverpool, bought at Christie's for £22 10s. od.

1917   Bequest by John Elliot of 44 pictures mostly by local Liverpool artists.

1923   Bequest by James Smith of Blundellsands of paintings by Watts, Monticelli, the Liverpool artists Windus and Williamson, and sculpture by Rodin.

1924–31   Public criticism and discussion of the shortcomings of the permanent collection, leading to a change in the Gallery's acquisition policy. Letter from Councillor H.R.Rathbone to Henry Cole, Chairman of Libraries, Museum and Arts Committee, criticizing the acquisition policy of the Walker Art Gallery and the unrepresentative nature of the permanent collection; 1929 first contribution from the rates to the picture purchase fund, £750; 1931 letter by Colonel Vere Cotton to *Liverpool Post and Courier* pointing out inadequacies of the permanent collection brought the debate to a head.

1931–32   Gallery closed for reconstruction and extension, partly paid for by gifts and bequest from George Audley, F.C.Browing and Thomas Bartlett, each of £10,000.

1932   Bequest by George Audley of 26 pictures by Clausen and others. One of the Gallery's major benefactors, he had given through his lifetime numerous pictures: by Wilkie, Linnell, Leighton, Wyllie and others.

1933   Gallery reopened. Opening Exhibition included pictures by Picasso and Gauguin. Bequest by Lord Wavertree of £20,000 and his collection of British paintings.

1934   Unit one Exhibition. Included Barbara Hepworth, Henry Moore, Paul Nash.

1935   *Snowdon from Llyn Nantlle* by Richard Wilson bought for £950.

1939–49   Taken over by Ministry of Food. Collections dispersed. Exhibitions organized at Bluecoat Chambers.

1943   *Mrs Mounter* by Harold Gilman bought for £550.

1944   Bequest by Emma Holt, of Sudley together with her father's collection, to the City of Liverpool.

1945   Exhibition of *Recent Acquisitions* at the National Gallery, London.

1948   William Roscoe's Collection and other pictures presented by the Liverpool Royal Institution acting jointly with the University.

1950–51   Sudley opened May 1950. Gallery reopened after some re-construction, July 1951. *Festival of Britain* Exhibition on George Stubbs.

1951–53   To mark the reopening a series of important pictures presented by local commerce and industry including, *Molly Longlegs Held by her Jockey* by George Stubbs given by Messrs Lewis's Limited, 1951. *Self Portrait* by Rembrandt given by the Managers of the Ocean Steam Ship Company (P.H.Holt Trust).

1955   Vincent Van Gogh Exhibition, an outstanding success. Staff expanded and wider programme of activities begun, including development of Education Service.

1957   First *John Moores Liverpool Exhibition* jointly sponsored by John Moores and Libraries, Museums and Arts Committee – since held biennially.

1960   *The Virgin and Child with St. Elizabeth and the Child Baptist* by Rubens purchased with the aid of a Treasury Grant of £25,000 and contributions from trusts, firms and private individuals, for £50,000. Received the bequest of £35,000 from F.W.Mayor of Blundellsands, shared by the Walker Art Gallery and Liverpool Museums for the purchase of seventeenth and eighteenth century sculpture and decorative arts.

1961   Special appeal to industry and commerce on Merseyside to enable nineteenth century and modern pictures to be bought. Over £70,000 contributed. Paintings by Degas, Seurat, Monet, Courbet, Cézanne and others have been purchased with the aid of the fund. Appeal renewed 1968, over £40,000 received.

1963   Air conditioning installed in Rooms 1, 2, and 3. First of new series of comprehensive catalogues published on the Foreign Schools.

1964   Exhibition of the work of Ford Madox Brown as first of three exhibitions re-assessing Pre-Raphelite artists. Millais 1967, Holman Hunt 1969.

1971   First *Peter Moores Liverpool Project* jointly sponsored by Peter Moores and the Libraries, Museums and Arts Committee – since held biennially.

1972   Bequest by C.F.J.Beausire of his collection of Early English Watercolours. 278,102 visitors, a post-war record.

1974   Walker Art Gallery transferred from Liverpool Corporation to the Merseyside County Council. Important Government long term loan of three paintings formerly in the Earl of Sefton's collection at Croxteth, near Liverpool, notably Gainsborough's *Viscountess Molyneux*.

1978   The Lady Lever Art Gallery, Port Sunlight, transferred by its Trustees to the care of Merseyside County Council, with its superb collection of eighteenth century English furniture and paintings, Pre-Raphaelites and nineteenth century paintings, Wedgwood pottery and Oriental Blue and White. Publication of new illustrated catalogues: *Foreign Schools* and *Merseyside Painters, People and Places*.

1979   Allen Jones Retrospective exhibition, as the first of a new series on modern British painting.

J. M. W. Turner: **Rosenau**
in Sudley Art Gallery (see page 89)

Pictures in the Gallery

Christ Discovered in the Temple

Inscribed and dated:

SYMON. DE. SENIS. ME. PINXIT. SUB. A.D.M.C. (CC) XL.II

49.5 × 35.1cm

From William Roscoe's collection

deposited by Liverpool Royal Institution 1893 and presented 1948

Sienese School
Simone Martini
c.1284–1344

In Simone's lifetime Siena produced many of the best painters in Italy. He was counted among the greatest of them. His patrons included the King of Naples and the Pope, for whom he went to work at Avignon. It was there that he painted this picture, which is one of his very few surviving late works, and this Gallery's most valued possession. In the gold and diapered frame which is an integral part of the picture he has inscribed his name and the date: Simone of Siena painted me in 1342.

The elaborate Gothic arch of the frame, the punched decoration, the enamel colours, all combine to give the effect of a glittering tabernacle, suggesting the Temple itself; and within it, the golden background conveys a sense of infinite depth beyond the three holy figures.

After Christ's dispute with the Doctors in the Temple his parents found him there and Mary asked him: 'Son, why hast thou thus dealt with us? Behold thy father and I have sought thee, sorrowing'. 'How is it that ye sought me? Wist ye not that I must be about my Father's business?' Christ replied. The story occurs in St Luke's gospel and Mary's question appears in the Latin of the Vulgate on the book she holds. The subject is very rare.

Simone brings out the human drama of the story. The telling gesture of Joseph drawing Christ towards the questioning Mary is accentuated by the flowing attitudes and curving draperies. In contrast Christ stands stiff and erect, his hands folded defiantly, asserting his independence. The emotions of the three characters are brilliantly portrayed in their faces – particularly that of St Joseph, with his expression of pained reproach; the way in which the silhouette of his mantle focuses attention on his eyes intensifies its poignancy.

At this period, tempera was used for panel painting: the pigment was mixed with an emulsion, often glue or egg. Tempera was inherently less versatile than oil, but has been used here by Simone with the greatest refinement. Many of the colours were required by convention: gold, for instance, was always used for the background of sacred pictures, and Mary's robe was always blue. But Simone has chosen the colours to form a satisfying harmony. The reddish tinge of the gold makes the reds of the garments more resonant. The lilac of Joseph's mantle mediates between the reds and the blues of Mary and Christ, and is one of the most memorable colours in Italian mediaeval painting.

Detail. (see colour plate, page ii)

Pietà

About 1490–1496
34.3×31.1cm
From William Roscoe's collection
deposited by Liverpool Royal Institution 1893
and presented 1948

Ferrarese School
Ercole de' Roberti
c.1450–1496

This was originally part of a predella, the set of small panels usually placed below an Italian altarpiece. It hung in the church of S. Giovanni in Monte, Bologna, between two other panels which are now in Dresden.

They record events from Christ's Passion: but in our panel the historical event, the Crucifixion, has been set in the background, while in the foreground there is a *Pietà* – the Virgin alone mourning the dead Christ – for which there is no source in the Bible. It was intended to illustrate two of the dominant themes of Catholic thought: the Virgin's motherly love for her Son (which she feels also for us), and our Saviour's suffering for our salvation. In this painting, then, we are invited to share her grief, and to feel outrage at the Crucifixion.

Ercole's means are peculiarly appropriate for this subject. Christ's body is drawn and wasted, a masterpiece of expressive anatomy. His head is seen from a most unusual angle – brilliantly foreshortened – to suggest the distorted features of a dead man. The outlines of the figures are hard and angular – an aspect of much Ferrarese art, which Ercole here uses with great poignancy. The Virgin and Christ appear starkly prominent with the Crucifixion painted sketchily in pastel tones in a hazy distance. The colours of the whole are sombre: the Virgin's robe is black instead of the conventional blue. The pink living flesh of the Virgin's hand is set against the yellowish dead flesh of Christ's. There is a powerful contrast between the strident emotion of the side panels, and the stillness of grief in the centre.

It is painted mostly in oil, which was a medium introduced from Northern Europe towards the end of the fifteenth century and made possible soft lustrous surfaces and more delicate transitions of colour. Here it is used with great delicacy, for example, in the painting of Christ's chest and the translucent veil of the Virgin; while the highlights have been painted in the older medium of tempera (Colour plate on p. 6).

(see colour plate, page 6)

Virgin and Child

37.8×36.5cm
Purchased with the aid of the Special Appeal Fund
the Mayor Bequest, the NACF, the Pilgrim Trust and
a Grant-in-aid from the Victoria and Albert Museum
1978

Venetian School

Bartolommeo Montagna

Active 1459–1523

The painter of this intimate religious study of the Virgin and Child with a devotee was one of the distinguished Northern Italian artists of the Renaissance. He was trained at Venice in the circle of the renowned Giovanni Bellini and was afterwards, from 1475 until his death, principally active in nearby Vicenza, where this was probably painted in the later 1480s.

Unlike many larger works of the period, this tiny panel was never meant to grace the altar of a church, but was intended for individual meditation and devotion. The figures take up the maximum space and the spectator is brought very close to them, but rather as a looker on than as a participant, for the Virgin looks not to us but towards the young bearded man who kisses the Child's feet. The young man occupies that part of the picture often reserved for the donor and he has been identified with a possible patron of Montagna's, Francesco Gonzaga, the Marquess of Mantua. However, he bears the remains of a halo, wears the hair shirt, hair and beard associated with representations of St John the Baptist, and this identification is the more likely.

The landscape beyond the parapet at the left with a path twisting past houses towards a distant expanse of water, is a more spiky development of the gently rolling landscapes of Bellini; but the agressive rocky outcrop at the right, closing off the composition, is nearer to the Paduan school of Mantegna and typical of Montagna's own development. The colouring is glowing but muted with a telling contrast between the silvery blues of the Virgin's robes and the pale flesh tints set against the warm browns of the landscape. We are made aware of the subtlety in handling of colour and tone which was the hallmark of the Venetian School.

The Entombment

55.2×56.3cm

Deposited by Liverpool Royal Institution 1893
and presented 1948

Netherlandish School

Master of the Virgo inter Virgines

Active 1480–1495

Early painters seldom signed their works. In the absence of documents they therefore often remain anonymous. The Master of the Virgo inter Virgines is so known because of a painting by him of this subject, *The Virgin amongst Virgins*, in Amsterdam. The artist was a Dutchman, probably from Delft, active in the later fifteenth century. Although his name has been lost his personality speaks clearly through his style. The attenuated figures with their long necks, skull-like heads and thin expressive hands are characteristic of his work. Such brutal realism appears to be typical of Dutch art of the period, as distinct from the more idealized productions of the Flemish masters of the Southern Netherlands. Unfortunately, the vast majority of Late Mediaeval Dutch panel paintings were destroyed during the religious strife of the sixteenth and seventeenth centuries. For this reason, this surviving painting is all the more precious.

The artist has chosen the moment between the deposition from the cross and the entombment, when the body of Christ is brought to his mother. In the foreground, identifiable by his rich clothing, is Joseph of Arimathaea, the wealthy disciple who begged Jesus's body from Pilate and 'laid it in his own new tomb'. He is assisted by Nicodemus and by Mary Magdalene, who walks behind looking sorrowfully over Christ's head directly at the Virgin. The splendour of her costume and that of her companions emphasizes the stark simplicity of the dead Christ. St John supports the Virgin as she kneels in agonized prayer contemplating the exhausted corpse of her son. Behind them stand the two holy women whose helpless gestures serve as a 'dramatic chorus' to the poignancy of the central action. In the background, behind the boulders, another figure removes one of the ladders with which Christ's body has been taken from the cross.

The two distinct groups of figures are drawn together by telling compositional devices, notably the diagonals created by Joseph stepping forward balanced by St John's outstretched left foot, by the drooping arm of Christ, and by the clasped hands of the women. The wavelike pathway indicates the way towards the tomb, to which the woman at the left, unable to look at the dead Christ, already half turns.

The artist was skilled in the handling of the opalescent and translucent qualities of Netherlandish oil techniques. This is particularly apparent in the precise observation of the brocade, fur, gauze and jewellery of Joseph's elaborate costume which contrasts so strongly with the pasty monochrome of Christ's dead body. The greyish-brown tones of the background provide a muted backdrop to the stronger foreground colours, and emphasizes the sombre theme.

Portrait of a Young Man
About 1520
96.6×73.7cm
From William Roscoe's collection
deposited by Liverpool Royal Institution 1893
and presented 1948

Netherlandish School
Jan Mostaert
c.1475–1555/6

A young man appears in an attitude of prayer before a landscape in which may be seen the legend of St Hubert.

St Hubert went out hunting on a holy day when such activities were forbidden. The stag he was chasing suddenly turned round and Hubert saw that it had a crucifix between its horns: confronted with this miracle he fell on his knees to worship it and to repent of his sin. No doubt this saint must have had some personal significance for the sitter: for example his name may have been Hubert.

The religious context of this portrait is a reminder that pure portraiture was a fifteenth century development of the portraits of donors in religious pictures (for instance in our *Crucifixion* triptych by the Master of the Aachen Altarpiece, seen when the wings are closed).

The presentation of the young man's personality is unemphatic but effective, as are other aspects of the picture. Attention is drawn to his head by its silhouetting against the sky, and from it we may read his character, mild but serious. Mostaert was a court painter, and often portrayed his sitters in smart clothes, to which he devoted as much attention as to the face. Here he conveys differences of sheen and texture with great sublety, and picks out even the young man's unusual form of glove, which allows the ring to show through.

The background contains a wonderful variety of life: a gaily dressed group of courtiers has come down for a picnic from a walled town, with a Negro groom and a huntsman who is blowing his horn. Two whippets are reflected in the water as they drink. Curiously blasted trees and the walled town dominate the landscape, which is linked to the young man by a rough stone wall serving as his prayer desk. Above, there is a spacious watery sky, like that of Holland: from it emerges the sun, a symbol of God.

Browns, brownish greens, and related colours predominate. Bluish greys produce an important subsidiary note. The result – a basically 'brown' picture with rather a cool tonality – shows that ability to characterize a picture in terms of a single colour and a restricted range of tones, which is one of the great achievements of sixteenth century painting.

The Nymph of the Fountain

Inscribed and dated:

FONTIS NYMPHA SACRI SOMNUM NE RVMPE QVIESCO/1534

50.8×76.2cm

Deposited by Liverpool Royal Institution 1893, and presented 1948

German School

Lucas Cranach the Elder

1472–1553

Cranach was one of the greatest names in the great period of German painting in the first half of the sixteenth century. This period was one of great stylistic upheaval, in which a number of artists followed the classicizing path which Albrecht Dürer had recently driven through the northern Late Gothic heritage. Although Cranach and his contemporaries were, in a sense, transitional artists, such a term does little justice to their immense powers of invention.

The variety of Cranach's cultural heritage is apparent in the sources upon which he drew in this painting. The basic theme of the sleeping nymph was transmitted from Italy, probably via a woodcut in the famous Venetian illustrated book, the *Hypnerotomachia Poliphili* of 1499. Dürer took up the idea in 1514. In a drawing of that year, he depicted the sleeping nymph before a fountain with a classical inscription, as an illustration to a pseudo-antique legend. According to this story, there was in the region of the Danube an enchanted spring above which was carved the figure of its guardian nymph, together with an inscription forbidding the passer-by to disturb her. Cranach himself first treated the subject in a drawing and a painting of 1515. These contain all the essential ingredients of the Liverpool picture, painted nineteen years later.

The identity of the nymph is deliberately equivocal. Whilst the partridges are a symbol of Venus, the bow and arrows are common both to the goddess of love and to the chaste Diana, the goddess of hunting.

Cranach has created a remarkably powerful erotic image. For while the Latin text on the fountain reads: 'I am resting, the nymph of the sacred spring. Do not awaken me', the attitude of the nymph contradicts this. Her half-opened eyes, which glance candidly outwards at the observer, and her languid smile suggest invitation. This impression is intensified by the presence of the rumpled stripey pillow – a quite unclassical element. The veil clings and conceals nothing. The soft grassy bank silhouettes her pale body which contrasts breathtakingly with the deep blue of the sky. The bulging basin of the fountain reiterates the sinuous curves of the nymph, just as the apples, ripe for the picking, reiterate the form of her breasts. Exuberant cupids spurting water in the fountain underline the artist's ironical comment on the classical myth.

Queen Elizabeth I
'The Pelican Portrait'
About 1574
78.7×61cm
Presented by E. Peter Jones, 1945

Style of
Nicholas Hilliard
1547–1619

Portraits have always formed a significant proportion of English paintings. This was particularly so in the Tudor epoch when few other subjects were commissioned. They were often used for political purposes and were given as gifts to foreign princes, leading statesmen or relatives. According to family tradition this portrait was given by the Queen to the Howards, one of the most powerful families of the day (in the same way our picture of Henry VIII belonged to the Seymours).

At this date relatively few artists' names are known with the striking exception of the foreigner Holbein, court painter to Henry VIII, and the court painters to Elizabeth, Gower and the miniaturist, Hilliard. This portrait comes close in style to Hilliard's, who is known to have painted 'in large'.

English portraits at this time recorded the sitters' status rather than their personality, and conveyed their achievements, interests and position through multiple symbolism. In this they echo the characteristics of European painting of the period, in particular the Italian Mannerist School. The Queen is treated almost like a religious icon, a stylized image in sumptuous array in isolated majesty. Her waxlike complexion is partly explained by the fact that painters were forbidden to show shadows on her face, since she considered these to be blemishes. Solidity and the breath of life come rather from the shadow thrown on the back of the canopy under which she stands, from the naturalistic rose at her bosom and cherries at her ear, and from the almost tangible reality of the dewy pearls cascading over her dress.

Many of the details of Elizabeth's costume are significant. The very elaborate jewelled fan which she holds in her right hand is of the type presented to her annually by the City Fathers. The rose and fleur-de-lys behind her head signify her claims to the British and French thrones. The Tudor Rose is embodied in the blackwork embroidery of her sleeves and a real rose is tucked into the right of her bodice. The thornless rose was a symbol of the Virgin Mary, and hence of Virginity. Just as Mary was married to the Church so the Virgin Queen was married to her country.

On her breast is the pendant that gives the portrait its name. The pelican which pecked at its breast to feed its children with its own blood is a symbol of Christ's work of redemption and sacrifice, and of his Resurrection. Hence in this context it came to mean Elizabeth as nurse and mother of the Church in England.

Self-Portrait

About 1630
72.3 × 57.7cm
Presented by Ocean Steam Ship Company
(P.H.Holt Trust), 1953

Dutch School
Rembrandt van Rijn
1606–1669

Rembrandt's fame now obscures his unconventionality. Unlike other Dutch painters, he touched practically every type of subject. He made great innovations in technique, handling of colour, and treatment of his subject matter. His works show a developing force of personality exceptional in European painting.

He painted more self-portraits than any other painter, probably to study ways of conveying states of mind by exterior means – one of a painter's most difficult tasks. His self-portraits are remarkable for their precise characterization of his changing personality. The earliest show a forceful, rather uncouth young man: this one, painted when he was about 24, belongs to a slightly later development. Still self-assertive, he bears signs of intelligence and good humour; well dressed, he is almost a respectable bourgeois.

Rembrandt's use of lighting is highly original, though still immature: dramatic and concentrated, but somewhat improbable. It picks out Rembrandt's cheek as the centre of a design based on ovals and the curves of his chain. It distracts attention from the broadness of his face, and the fullness of his lips: it flatters him, in fact. It conveys a sense of the surrounding atmosphere, by allowing the form of his head to dissolve into the enveloping shade. It leaves the eyes, to which one naturally looks in a portrait, in shadow. One has, then, to make an effort in reading his expression; and that effort involves one in the picture.

At this period of his career, Rembrandt uses extremely subdued greys and browns; but he delights in differences of texture – in the contrast, for instance, between the thickly-painted highlights of the cheek and the softness of the hair.

This self-portrait was probably in King Charles I's collection by 1633 – a sign of Rembrandt's early reputation. In fact he soon had many followers, from whose works in this Gallery something of his development may be seen. *The Angel Appearing to Hagar* deals with the human themes of sympathy, charity and forgiveness, which were dear to Rembrandt and his followers. A sense of homeliness is conveyed by the peasant types of the two actors. By far the most sensitive is the *Portrait of a Man* by Carel Fabritius (1622 – 1654), which reflects Rembrandt's later style in its pasty paint and broken brushwork, its warm tones – especially the tawny orange – and its sympathy for human misfortune.

Virgin and Child
with St Elizabeth and the Child Baptist
About 1632–1634
180 × 139.5cm
Purchased with the aid of a Treasury grant
and contributions from trusts, firms and private individuals
1960

Flemish School
Peter Paul Rubens
1577–1640

Rubens was the foremost painter in Flanders in the seventeenth century. He excelled in compositions at once lively and harmonious, in richness of colour and vivacity of handling, in warmth of feeling for a well-fed, vital humanity. He was widely patronized by the courts of Europe. St Elizabeth was the mother of John the Baptist and a cousin of the Virgin. Paintings of this moving family event became very popular. The presence of St Joseph was optional, as also was the lamb. Lambs had been used for sacrifice in Israel: the lamb here signifies Christ's acceptance of his own sacrifice on the cross. The painting probably served as an altarpiece.

St Joseph, who appeared by the column in an earlier stage of the design recorded in a contemporary engraving, has been painted out to emphasize the central group. Light plays on the soft bright flesh of the Madonna and golden-haired Child, and on the contrasting weathered St Elizabeth and suntanned St John. The vivid colours of the Virgin are contrasted with the earthy darker hues of the two worshippers. The figures are bulkier than those we have seen so far: their slightest movement seems powerful. Massive architecture adds to the majesty of the scene. It is softened by the evanescent shimmer of the landscape, glimpsed in the background, from which St Elizabeth and St John appear to have emerged to worship along with the spectator.

Rubens conveys here the excitement of an instant. The heads and eyes of the Virgin and Child are sharply turned, in positions that could be held only for a moment; in a second St John will have kissed Christ's foot. Broad, flickering brushwork suggests the movement of the draperies.

Rubens thought with his brush: the basic design changed as the picture developed. The presence of St Joseph by the column had emphasized a disturbing diagonal. The Virgin's aquamarine robe was subtly touched with mauve to assert the importance of the Christ Child. There is now a tension between impetuous movement and perfect balance of design. The movement is precariously suspended, the instant prolonged.

River Scene with Ferry Boat

Signed and dated 1650
106×152cm
Bequeathed by E.E.Cook
through the National Art Collections Fund
1955

Dutch School
Salomon van Ruysdael
1602–1670

Seventeenth century art in Holland was unlike art in the Catholic countries. Since Holland was predominantly Protestant, there was little demand for sacred pictures and artists tended to be highly specialized. Ruysdael, for instance, painted chiefly landscapes. From the previous century, Dutch artists had learned to look keenly at their surroundings, and paint what they found there.

In the early 1600s Dutch landscapists began to approach their subject in a new way. They found in the moist atmosphere of Holland, the great expanse of sky over flat rolling country, the canals disappearing into hazy distance, the pale tonalities of their northern country, a means of painting atmospheric landscape. The result was quite unlike that of the previous century when abrupt changes of colour and tone were used to convey distance and there was no sense of the continuity of light.

Ruysdael's very characteristic painting shows a mature development of this new feeling. It is concerned first with weather: we sense the massed clouds moving as the sun reappears after rain. The clear light allows a broad range of colour and contrast in the blues and greys and greens. The haze still lingers in grey and creamy streaks over the canal which reflects its colours as it disappears diagonally into the distance, while the foreground is thrown into heavy dark green and brown shadows beneath the bright sky, attracting our attention back to the land. A bulky tree in full leaf dominates the centre. To its left is the light watery distance of the canal, but a ferry boat prevents our eye sweeping too swiftly to the horizon. On the right a great barn and dovecote with pyramidal roof draws attention down to the lively details below, where sunlight sparkles on leaves partially masked by shadow and people go about their everyday tasks.

For this is the second preoccupation of the artist – the objective observation of his contemporaries doing ordinary things. They ferry their cattle across to market at the town whose church spire appears in softer colours beyond the trees. They set fishing nets, carry goods about, just talk. They are drawn into a vision of gently moving, ever changing nature, in a composition seemingly simple but really extremely complex.

Italian School
Giovanni Paolo Panini
1691/2−1765

This is not a view of Rome but an arbitrary rearrangement of some of the most famous buildings of ancient Rome, rather like a photomontage. On the right is the column of Trajan, dedicated in A.D.113, showing the events of Trajan's wars in Rumania. In the centre is an obelisk with the emblems of Seti I and Rameses II, which Octavian had conveyed from Egypt after the victory of Actium over Antony and Cleopatra in 31 B.C. Slightly to the left is the Pantheon, erected by Hadrian between A.D.118 and 128, which exerted an exceptional influence on European architecture of the sixteenth to the eighteenth centuries. All the buildings are shown in their state of preservation in the artist's day.

The buildings are solidly disposed, with a calculated variety that probably owes something to stage scenery. There is a fine balance between archaeology and atmosphere – both of which Panini's patrons wanted. Many of them were wealthy Englishmen, whose visit to Rome on their Grand Tour was the high point of their education. They had been taught to admire the monuments of classical antiquity, and enjoyed them as ruins: for the remains demonstrated the transience of even the greatest of earthly things, and encouraged an agreeable mood of poetic melancholy. A similar experience of the ruins inspired Gibbon to write *The Decline and Fall of the Roman Empire*. In this picture the mood is well conveyed by the calm evening light, by the absence of modern habitation, and by the classically-dressed figures, philosophically surveying the ruins of their own civilization.

The antique statue on the left now in the Museo Nazionale, Naples, indicates the importance of sculpture in the eighteenth century conception of antiquity. English collectors brought back both classical works and recent Italian works in a classical style. One of the finest of such collections was formed by Henry Blundell of Ince (1723/4−1810), some of which is now displayed in this Gallery and the Museum. At Ince Blundell Hall the collection was housed in a specially designed rotunda based on the Roman Pantheon.

David Garrick as Richard III

Painted in 1745
190.5×250.8cm
Purchased with the aid of the National Art Collections Fund
and the Wavertree Fund, 1956

William Hogarth
1697–1764

Hogarth began his career when foreign artists were gaining many of the most important commissions in Britain. He spent much of his life trying to demonstrate 'that contemporary British art was equal to that of the old masters' – and chose subjects from the English theatre and moralizing scenes of everyday life rather than Italian poetry and classical mythology.

David Garrick was a personal friend of Hogarth's. He collected his paintings and dedicated a play to him. His first performance in London in Lincoln's Inn Fields as Richard III won him high acclaim. He was the first English actor to wear historical costume, and his innovations in the theatre are comparable with Hogarth's approach to painting.

Hogarth chose the key moment in the Tent Scene (Act V scene 3), where the King awakes from his sleep still staring with wild eyes at the ghosts of those whom he has destroyed. They have warned him of the retribution awaiting him at the Battle of Bosworth that morning. Whilst his soldiers are calmly warming themselves at the fire outside their tents, the King in panic thrusts out his hand to ward off the vision. The great scale of the picture matches the grandeur of the theme and exemplifies Hogarth's attempt to create a mature English school of history painting. The robes are beautifully painted with thick silky brush strokes, and the reflections in the armour are a typical tour de force.

The head of Garrick is painted from life on a smaller canvas which was later set into the rest of the picture – the seam shows. The effect of the hand reaching at us is achieved by brilliant foreshortening. The King gropes forward into the light from the frightening shadows surrounding him.

The sweeping lines of the tent curtain and robes emphasize his mental and physical isolation. Significant details are introduced at either end, the crucifix symbolizing the God whom he has forsaken, the crown that he is to lose that day and the armour that he is to wear in the battle, while a piece of paper quotes the words in Shakespeare's play:

Jockey of Norfolk be not so bold
For Dickon, thy master is bought and sold.

a reference to the treachery of Lord Stanley, who unlike the loyal Duke of Norfolk, changed sides at the start of the battle.

The fine English craftsmanship of the elaborately carved frame with its crown of trophies, should also be noted (Colour plate p.10).

Molly Longlegs
About 1760–1762
101 × 126.8cm
Presented by Messrs Lewis's Ltd, 1951

George Stubbs
1724–1806

George Stubbs, the most famous Liverpool-born artist, was England's greatest animal painter. During the eighteenth century pictures of hunting scenes, of races, and of favourite horses became increasingly popular with the English gentry. Into the world of the humdrum journeyman painter Stubbs brought a personal insight into character, derived from his early pre-occupation with portraiture, and an outstanding knowledge of the anatomy of the horse, which he studied with tenacity over a period of years. His paintings thus rise above those of his contemporaries in their characterization and reality as well as in their mastery of composition and delicacy of colour. His interests coincided with the new scientific attitude to livestock breeding and agriculture.

Molly Longlegs was a mare bred by Fulke Greville of Wilbury House, Wiltshire in 1753. She raced for Mr Greville between 1757 and 1761 and for Lord Bolingbroke in 1761 and 1762. This picture was exhibited in 1762 with a companion picture of another of Lord Bolingbroke's horses.

It is an individual portrait of a particular horse. Not only her extra long legs but the slight turn of her head, the rolling eyes, are expressive of personality; her jockey catches at her reins to hold her still for a moment. The jockey too is a straight portrait, and like the saddle and girth thrown casually to one side, illustrates Stubbs' acute observation of everyday things.

The background is idealized with broad planes of colour in sky, hill and river, to provide a setting that does not distract attention from the bolder lines and brighter colours of the horse and her jockey.

Isabella, Viscountess Molyneux, later Countess of Sefton

1768/9
236×155cm
From the Earls of Sefton at Croxteth;
presented by H.M.Government, 1975

Thomas Gainsborough
1727–1788

Isabella Stanhope, daughter of the 2nd Earl of Harrington, married in 1768 Charles William Viscount Molyneux, afterwards 1st Earl of Sefton. At the time of her marriage she sat to several artists and by far the most important of her portraits is this by Gainsborough, painted during his years at Bath (1759–1774) during his rise to prominence as the chief and only rival of Sir Joshua Reynolds.

This dashing likeness of the bride happily balances the informal naturalness characteristic of Gainsborough's earlier work from his days in East Anglia under the influence of Dutch and French painting, and the formal demands of his increasingly aristocratic patrons. His style was totally at variance with the classicizing Grand Manner in the influential full-length public portraits promoted by his contemporary Reynolds. His matured technique likewise, with its conscious brushstrokes, embraced every texture and the whole surface of the picture and left nothing to drapery painters. Inspiration came at Bath from the elegant bravura paintings of Van Dyck which he was now able to see and which epitomized the aristocratic ideal.

Here in the bloom of her youth, Isabella stands firmly in an airy space, neither too formal nor too easy in her half-natural, half-conscious pose, and stepping lightly forward from the essentially artificial romanticized misty landscape. The white satin of her dress shimmers with glancing light. The contrasting textures of its lace, of the pearls, of the darker shawl, which acts as a foil to her graceful hands, set off the glowing creams and pinks of her complexion. The subdued brown sketchiness of the surrounding landscape with its characteristic broad brushstrokes, emphasizes her elegant dress and aristocratic pose.

It was such paintings as this, shown in 1769 at the first exhibition of the Royal Academy, of which he was a founder member, that gained Gainsborough his place at the height of eighteenth century English painting.

Snowdon from Llyn Nantlle

Before 1774
101 × 127cm
Purchased 1935

Richard Wilson
1714–1782

Wilson was born and died near the mountains of North Wales. He was very fond of painting his native country, particularly Snowdon and the area around the valley of the Mawddach. The picturesqueness of this part of Britain had only recently been discovered and artists and gentlemen in the late eighteenth century began to visit it much as they visited the hills south of Rome on the Grand Tour.

The artist had himself studied in Italy and this painting in fact shares many features with paintings of the Roman Campagna, and uses the same classical formula. A fundamentally balanced composition, almost decorative in its simplicity is framed by trees. These not only define the position from which we view the distant scene, but act with a delicate branch of leaves, as a bridge across the sky. Two more solid wings of low hills have been formed out of the natural scenery to create an inner frame for the far off peak of Snowdon. Their curves are counterbalanced in the reflections in the nearer lake, which itself frames the three tiny central figures.

The sense of scale and distance is created by clearly defined blocks of colour rather than misty atmosphere. The basically cool scheme is enlivened by the three figures in the centre foreground: two fishermen, one in a canary jacket, and a lady in a white shawl and blue dress of almost Japanese elegance. Further touches of colour are provided by browns, reds and whites in the little boats on what might otherwise have been a large empty expanse of water.

Exceptional in the artist's work is the concentration on landscape with a mountain as the focal point. No intruding building appears. Classically composed though the painting is, the artist has remained faithful to the true aspect of the mountains as seen from the far side of Llyn Nantlle. (The second lake has now been obliterated by a slate quarry, but was still visible in the 1930s.) He does, however, dramatize the sheerness of the slope on the left, accentuate the sharpness of the ridge on the right, and give greater prominence to Snowdon itself.

Wilson bathes his scenery in the warm sunlight of Italy. This together with the presence of figures creates an hospitable and Arcadian atmosphere.

Firework Display at the Castel Sant' Angelo

After 1774
140.3 × 172cm
Presented by Robert Neilson, 1880

Joseph Wright of Derby
1734–1797

Wright was the first artist of distinction to spend most of his life in the provinces. At Derby he was surrounded by a spirit of enquiry among his manufacturing friends and patrons, who included Wedgwood, the potter, and Arkwright, the cotton spinner. The same spirit of enquiry at the dawn of the Industrial Revolution inspired the subjects of many of Wright's paintings.

He was led in particular to study unusual conditions of lighting. His aim was part evocative, resulting in moonlight scenes like *The Lady in Comus* and in the early morning light of the *Convent of San Cosimato,* and part descriptive, causing him to choose events in real life such as the *Firework Display* which justified exceptional lighting effects.

Wright like many of his contemporaries, visited Italy. There, in 1774, he found an ideal subject in the firework display at Castel Sant' Angelo in Rome. He was fascinated by the parabolas of the rockets which gave the event its title, the Girandola. It was a regular spectacle for visitors and prompted comparisons with volcanic eruptions. Wright, in fact, painted at least three pairs of paintings of this subject coupled with an eruption of Vesuvius.

In his painting involvement of the spectator rather than topographical accuracy was the prime consideration. As in the Panini, several monuments are included which could not have been seen at the same time – Trajan's Column and the Pantheon find a place, whilst the Castel and St Peter's are brought closer to the spectator. Overriding is the artist's determination to capture the image of the spectacular flashing light of the yellow rockets momentarily highlighting fragments of the magnificent buildings in an orangey-pink glow.

Linlithgow Palace

Between 1802–1810
99×122.5cm
Presented by F.J.Nettlefold, 1948

Joseph Mallord William Turner
1775–1851

Views of castles and abbeys were produced in large numbers in the late eighteenth and early nineteenth centuries. Turner himself spent much of his early career touring Britain and sketching the scenery. He made his name as a topographical watercolourist. He made drawings of Linlithgow Palace on his tour of Scotland in 1801. This picture resulted and was exhibited at his own Gallery in 1810.

Compositionally it can be compared with Wilson's *Snowdon*. It too grows out of the classical tradition, while in its sense of atmosphere and hazy light and in the elaboration of secondary vistas it echoes Dutch landscape painters like Ruysdael and Van Goyen. The bathers provide areas of light in the foreground, while beyond them the sun catching the dark depths of the river leads the eye into its misty distant reaches. The sunlit town fragmentally seen on the right acts as a frame to the dense wooded bank of trees. The result is a highly elaborate composition, full of pictorial incident.

For Turner the effects of light, colour and atmosphere became far more important than accurate delineation of the topography. In this painting the pale evening sunlight glows pinky-brown on the castle and catches the silvery ripples on the water. Touches of red and yellow enliven the darkest area of the picture on the right, as does the white of the river shining through a gap in the trees.

In contrast to Wilson's clear-cut vision, a filmy atmosphere softens the silhouettes and envelops the distance. Turner later reduced his landscapes to atmospheric colour and light so that the forms of the rivers and hills became hard to distinguish. The untitled *Landscape* in the Collection shows his later style, in which traces of the framing trees are still visible, but the valley is wreathed in an orangey mist, under a pale white sky.

Blessing the Sea

Signed and dated 1876
76.5×127.3cm
Presented by George Audley, 1925

William Lionel Wyllie

1851–1931

Occasionally a minor artist produces a masterpiece and transcends his normal level of work. Wyllie was a marine painter who in his earlier work produced many objective clear-cut coastal and shipping views with a true sailor's understanding of the many moods of the sea translated into painterly terms. He later became a successful academician.

For a time he stayed on the north French coast and his youthful imagination was caught by this typical Breton subject. On a blustery day a 'Pardon' or religious pilgrimage is taking place, at which the local people accompany their priests and church choir in procession to the annual blessing of the sea on which they depend for their livelihood. It is an exciting occasion with the black and white of national costume in evidence, enhanced by the gay colours of personal ornaments and church banners, much singing and many spectators. Here it finally arrives at the beach below the sandhills, surging into a seething mass like a huge swarm, and twisting in sinuous curve towards the sea. The boisterous wind catching the banners, the cloaks and the streamers, emphasizes the winding movement of the crowd. The bright splashes of primary colours and black appear all the sharper against the softer tones of the sand and the pale wet light of the racing water. Around the edges of the swarm many tiny figures are picked out – a man hobbling on crutches, a boy leaning on an umbrella, a fashionable woman in a bustle. They are suggested with a minimum of brushwork and though the picture was worked up in the studio, not on the spot, the effect is reminiscent of contemporary Impressionism which seems to cast its spell on this artist working for a moment on French soil.

Signed and dated 1878
131×251.5cm
Purchased from Liverpool Autumn Exhibition
1878

William Frederick Yeames
1835–1918

A party of roundheads is interrogating the inhabitants of a manor house during the Civil War. The Royalist family await with baited breath the reply of the thoughtless boy to the question put to him. The titillating suspense has delighted audiences for a century.

Many stories have been invented for this picture, but the artist had no specific historical basis for it. He wrote:

> I had at the time I painted the picture, living in my house a nephew of an innocent and truthful disposition, and it occurred to me to represent him in a situation where the child's outspokenness and unconsciousness would lead to disastrous consequences, and a scene in a country house, occupied by the Puritans during the Rebellion in England, suited my purpose.

He set his stage like a theatre with the focus on the stiffly standing boy on whom all faces turn, his innocence underlined by the golden hair and silvery blue satin which distinguishes him from his drab and antique surroundings.

Pictures telling a story were at the height of their popularity in the later nineteenth century and a major attraction at the summer exhibitions of the Royal Academy and at the Liverpool Autumn Exhibitions which reflected them. Many were bought by the newly opening provincial galleries. The aim of the early managers of the Walker Art Gallery was to provide pictures of a popular character which 'by appealing to common feelings and sentiments of our daily life, have afforded a fine moral lesson, and given great pleasure to the numerous visitors . . . who are uninitiated in the higher forms of Art.'

Pictures such as this, unfortunately, all too often lacked any aesthetic quality. While appealing to the emotions in their subjects, they make no appeal for the sheer delight of colour and texture and form, which is such a fundamental quality in the work of their contemporaries in France, and indeed of art of all periods.

Nevertheless they have survived a century of constant display and endless reproduction and for this alone merit their place in the history of art and of taste.

Hope
66×53.3cm
Presented by James Smith (of Blundellsands)
1923

George Frederick Watts
1817–1904

The artist's sketch is a private thing. It can contain unexpected qualities which the final considered work may lack. His first ideas are often expressed with a freshness and verve of brushwork and form. The sketch can tell us much about the creative evolution of the composition. Moreover, taste today finds particular delight in its fluid tentative qualities where the imagination of the spectator is stimulated in a way which may form no part of the artist's intentions in his finished picture.

This sketch was given by Watts to a fellow exponent of High Art, the artist Lord Leighton. It dates from the 1870s and, in its symphonic scheme of blues and greens and the fine-drawn elongated figure balanced in rhythmic movement, echoes the contemporary trend of the Aesthetes for muted tones and delicate ethereal forms. The draperies of silk and gauze clinging in crinkled folds are reminiscent of the tiny Greek Tanagra sculptures then at the height of their popularity. Barely perceptible is the single white strand of the lyre, illuminated like a living note of music against the blurred blues of the background. The broken brush strokes, vividly real touches barely covering the canvas, add to the musical overtones of the conception.

This enchanting dreamy form is in fact the timeless figure of Hope. She appears blindfolded, solitary, in an empty vastness of desolation, resting quietly on the world and bowing low over her lyre from which she finds beauty in the note of the one remaining string. She epitomizes hope for humanity. The highly finished version, immensely popular, was part of the series of great allegories planned throughout Watts' career to uplift mankind and presented by him to the Nation.

A Street in Brittany
Signed and dated 1881
104.2 × 75.8cm
Purchased from Liverpool Autumn Exhibition
1882

Stanhope Forbes
1857–1947

Stanhope Forbes was the leader of a group of artists who, after finding their initial inspiration amongst the fisherfolk of Brittany, found at Newlyn in Cornwall a similar light and similar people amongst whom to find their subjects. Strongly influenced by the contemporary French social realists surrounding Bastien-Lepage, they sought to go back to nature and to paint the everyday life of simple people.

At the little fishing village of Cancale in Brittany in the early 1880s Forbes painted this picture as a first exercise in this 'plein air' concept. It shows the two characteristics which are present in all his later work and that of others of the Newlyn School. There is the cool, subdued, greyish-blue light, slightly blurred in outline but enlivened with sparkling touches of bright sunlight, which conjures up the soft fresh atmosphere of the Channel coasts; and secondly, the objective, undramatic recording of the ordinary doings of peasants or country people.

This records a momentary vision seen in passing a narrow street of cottages in the small port. Immediately before us a child in local dress stands prominently on the steps of her home, catching the brighter morning light outdoors to work at her netting. Beyond her womenfolk sit working at their doorsteps and exchange the news with a neighbour on her way to market. The men are all away at sea. The deliberate texture of the paint with broken brushstrokes unconcealed under 'high finish', not only helps to create the atmospheric envelope but also suggests movement – without, again, any sense of a still from a photograph.

Here is a use of colour, light, and texture in a manner which parallels the Impressionists but is still within the nineteenth century English artists' preoccupation with narrative content.

Ville d'Avray, White Houses

About 1882

33 × 46cm

Purchased with the aid of the Special Appeal Fund
the NACF, and a Grant-in-aid from the Victoria and Albert Museum
1961

French School
Georges Seurat
1859–1891

This sketch is one of Seurat's early works, still influenced by the Impressionists and set in the countryside near Paris which they loved. It shows how he develops their ideas for his own artistic ends. Set against the luxuriance of the cornfield, the farm buildings become the pretext for a study in abstract form and relationships of colour in bright sunlight.

The Impressionists were above all interested in light effects. Their interest had perhaps three main aspects. They wanted to create an *illusion* of what we actually see; but this became gradually less important in their painting. They wanted to paint in accordance with certain *scientific* views about colour: a given area is never composed of one colour, but of several; shadows are never black or grey, and white is never white, but both are always coloured. Finally, of course, they wanted their pictures to be *beautiful*: they believed that to achieve this they should emphasize the picture plane rather than recession from it, and they restricted themselves to a narrow range of colours and tones, which were generally light. A picture such as our Monet *Break-up of the Ice on the Seine, near Bennecourt*, of about 1893, is the outcome of these interests, though the illusionistic element is, by this date, reduced.

Seurat had no interest in producing illusions, but he was greatly preoccupied with scientific and aesthetic problems. *Ville d'Avray* is largely Impressionist in the application of its colour, but it already shows the beginning of a tendency towards 'Divisionism' – the separation of coloured areas into their constituent primary colours – for which he later became famous.

The painting has the clear articulation typical of Seurat, who avoided the loose texture and lack of form favoured by the Impressionists. He uses sharp contrasts of tone and of 'hot' colour to produce a firm grid of horizontals and verticals parallel to the picture plane. One house is placed squarely in the centre and other buildings almost symmetrically either side of it. The result is of extreme stability, even rigidity, with a concentration of focus which is typical of Seurat's landscapes.

Woman Ironing
About 1885
80×63.5cm
Purchased with the aid of the Special Appeal Fund, the NACF
and a Grant-in-aid from the Victoria and Albert Museum
1968

French School
Edgar Degas
1834–1917

In the second half of the nineteenth century new importance was attached to the painting of everyday life in place of classical subjects. Some painters brought out its bourgeois charms, and others used it as a vehicle for social and moral comment. No-one, however, took a more detached attitude towards it than did Degas, whose mature works emphasize the formal qualities of the people he depicts, to the exclusion of any sympathetic interest.

Laundresses and ballet dancers were among Degas' favourite subjects in the 1880s. Their rhythmical muscular movements fascinated him; yet by choosing moments when their arms or bodies were at their fullest stretch, he made them appear static, and thus appropriate for his curiously still compositions. He was probably influenced by snapshots in his apparently casual placing of the woman off-centre in this picture; but the emphasis given to diagonals at the bottom and to verticals at the left prevents the composition from seeming off-balance.

Here Degas is less concerned with the 'subject', a woman ironing, than with the effects of reflected light upon her in this particular action. Like so many of his later pictures, solid forms are dissolved into nebulous shadows or silhouettes blurred into or set against areas of light. The net curtain over the glass door softens the stream of yellow light from the room beyond, its lower edge fades into a greyish blue against the woodwork. The light catches on the arms, the hands, the back of the neck of the thin angular servant, intensifying the pressure of her arm upon the iron. The rough whitewashed wall sparkles dully. The pinks and blues of the woman's dress and the softer colours permeating her surroundings are enlivened by the shimmering green silk on the ironing board.

The sensitive brushwork and subtle modulations of colour and tone are influenced by Impressionist technique and by Degas' own use of pastel – the paint is visibly put on in places with the same furry strokes of soft colour.

This is one of a series in which Degas explored the many-sided possibilities of the exhausting action of ironing with his characteristic detached vision, in the same way that he looked at ballet dancers.

Sponsa de Libano
Signed and dated 1891
332.5×155.5cm
Purchased from Liverpool Autumn Exhibition,
1896

Edward Burne-Jones
1833–1898

Illustrating the 'Song of Solomon', Chapter IV, verses 8 and 16, where Solomon calls upon the North and South winds to blow upon his beloved, his bride of Lebanon (in Latin Sponsa de Libano) and waft her to him.

It epitomizes the 'Aesthetic Movement' of the later nineteenth century, the atmosphere of fragility, of langour and of sensuous melancholy, which Burne-Jones created. He was a young disciple of Rossetti (initially a Pre-Raphaelite) from whose mediaeval dream world his own style evolved, with the additional influence of the fifteenth century Florentine, Botticelli. With his friend William Morris he was also much concerned with designs for stained glass and other media.

The intial design for this picture was one of a series illustrating the 'Song of Solomon' made in the 1870s for embroideries. The passage it illustrates is one of the most voluptuous in the Bible but Burne-Jones has stressed the dream-like quality of it. The bride is hardly more tangible than the ethereal beings who waft her to her lover. The linear quality and elongated forms owe much to the study of Botticelli and also to the style he evolved for the window designs for the Morris firm with their long shapes and essentially flat decorative surfaces sharply outlined. Here too, mood and pattern have greater importance than solidity and the muted blues and greens carefully underline this quality. The movement of the Winds with their billowing drapery is brought back within the composition by the balanced uprights of the trees and figure, while reflected in the gently swaying bank of lilies, just caught in the barely perceptible draught of air. The medium is watercolour and tempera used with a similar fluidity, but affording greater transparency than the artist's oil paintings.

Bathers Dieppe

About 1902
131.4×104.5cm
Purchased 1935

Walter Richard Sickert

1860–1942

Sickert was a pupil of Whistler, through whom in 1883 he met the most important influence on his career, Degas. In 1885 he returned to France to Dieppe, which he was to visit frequently and finally to make his home from 1898 until 1903.

Bathers was one of several paintings of Dieppe subjects which were commissioned by a local cafe proprietor at 40 francs apiece as decoration for his restaurant. The patron, however, did not like the results and they were sold to a young American musician, later to be Consul in Dieppe. This series was Sickert's first exercise on a large scale. He had normally favoured a small format as for instance in our *Fancy Dress* or *The Gallery of the Old Bedford*.

The *Bathers* is unparalleled in Sickert's work, and indeed in any artist's paintings of a beach scene prior to this date. Previously in such subjects, part of the beach and the sky was invariably introduced. In *Bathers* the sea rises from the bottom to the top of the canvas, and there is no foreground or background. Like his friend Degas, he made great use of photographs, and painted scenes from unusual angles. But although the chosen view-point certainly suggests the influence of snapshots, the composition is extremely carefully worked out. In particular, the triple near-repetition of a bather produces an effect of movement from the lower right towards the less populated area of the canvas. The varied colours of the costumes, blue and white, red and white, and black, provide a lively contrast with the deep purple shallows in the foreground and the turquoise of the calmer waters beyond the breakers. The surge of the sea is conveyed by wavelike dashes, owing something to the Impressionists. By these means Sickert conveys in *Bathers* all the sparkle and movement of summer bathing.

Mrs Mounter
Painted 1916–1917
91.8×61.5cm
Wavertree Bequest Purchase,
1943

Harold Gilman
1876–1919

Harold Gilman was a close friend of Sickert. Both of them were members of the Camden Town Group – artists working in a district of North London, who like the Impressionists chose to paint everyday scenes. Gilman broke away from Sickert, since he abhorred his sombre tones, and adopted a brighter palette inspired by the brilliant colours of Van Gogh and Gauguin.

Very ordinary domestic scenes feature in many paintings of the early twentieth century in both England and France.

Mrs Mounter, Gilman's charlady, has weight and solidity. Gilman himself stated that one of his greatest ambitions was to capture the essence of a character in real life.

Mrs Mounter sits bolt upright, but perhaps a trifle timid, behind the outsize brown glazed teapot, looking at him with a gentle directness. In contrast to the pale restrained tones of the Vuillard, the near brutality of the colours brings out the homeliness of the sitter and intensifies the impression of her surroundings.

The interior of the dingy London house is transformed into a glowing kaleidoscope. An exciting pattern is made out of the commonplace tableware where the light sparkles from the teapot and the lustre jug and plays in a dozen colours over the thick white cups and plates. The ladderback chair throws a green shadow on the dingy brown woodwork which comes to life in a series of horizontal and vertical borders of tan and ochre with lavender seams, while the ancient wallpaper glows with turquoise brilliance. The paint, unlike that of the Impressionists, is thick and heavy following Gauguin and Van Gogh. There are large flat areas of colour as in *Under the Hammer*, our painting by his friend Robert Bevan. Most striking, Mrs Mounter's face is seen as a mosaic of deliberate patches of different pinks, browns, and greens, as her complexion catches reflected light from a source at the right. She is outlined and given prominence by a thick black contour which follows the line of the scarf tied round her grey hair. In spite of the artist's uncompromising vision of her his sympathetic understanding and respect for this simple old woman is apparent.

The Fever Van
Signed and dated 1935
43.1 × 53.3cm
Purchased 1943

L.S.Lowry
1887–1976

The grit and desolation of the industrial Northwest has become a subject of glowing colour and lively grey atmosphere under the sympathetic gaze of Lowry. His pictures of the small factory towns and the large industrial panoramas around Manchester have the detached familiarity of the native-born, not the earnestness of the social worker. He wrote to the Gallery:

> I have spent ever since 1919 on these Industrial Scenes, and don't seem able to get really interested in anything else. In fact if I was asked my chief recreations, I ought to say walking about the streets of a poor quarter of any place I may happen to be in.

Under his hand the enveloping grime becomes a silvery-grey light, the drab streets, the ugly Manchester brick, afford passages of glowing colour. His figures are manikins, his dogs matchsticks, but they suggest real people, real mongrels, going about their individual concerns. The workers appear essentially solitary, like the artist, but occasionally are drawn together by some common sympathy or neighbourly misfortune – the fever van was a common enough sight in the thirties.

Formal patterns emerge in this back-street scene, with the balancing lines of the houses, the regular pattern of windows, the bright spots of colour at each door and the masses of strong reds at either end counterbalancing each other. The street slowly merges away from the gently personal event at its centre into a blackish-grey framing the stylized church and factory chimney which loom with a sort of inevitability from the far end. These put a stop to the vista and localize the inhabitants just as the four bollards strategically cut off escape in the foreground and prevent also our nearer participation.

Lowry's subjects were seldom exact accounts of particular places but were worked up in the studio. He sought for the essence of the Northern scene, not the particular. His near 'primitive' vision has made out of this black spot a subject of pride and enjoyment, not shame and derision, and this is perhaps the fundamental reason for his popularity in a world still taken up with abstract ideas.

Landscape of the Moon's Last Phase

Painted 1943–1944
63.5×75.8cm
Presented by the Contemporary Art Society
1947

Paul Nash
1889–1946

The early 1930s saw a re-awakening of interest in nineteenth century Romantic English landscape painting and the emergence of a new school of landscape artists. Paul Nash combined an imaginative approach to the English scene with elements of abstract and surrealist art to arrive ultimately at a highly personal interpretation of landscape as a symbolic form.

The war years too saw much evidence of a romantic evocation of the past overlaid with fear for the future. Nash was little interested in the mere reproduction of actual things but explored their hidden implications. He looked for evidence in the visible world of the phenomena of early Man. He found in the interplay of land and sky, and sun and moon symbols of life and death. We are barely conscious that his haunted landscapes are devoid of human form.

This painting is one of a series dating from the artist's final years concerned with the theme of the solstice and the equinox, which fascinated him as it had primitive peoples. It is a re-creation of a prospect of Wittenham Clumps in Berkshire, viewed from a house he often visited and which had profoundly fascinated him from his childhood. The primeval earth-works of man's earliest creation are seen in a close communion with the airy spaces of the sky and the fading moon. The tangled undergrowth is tinged with the browns of autumn; greyblue mists rise noiselessly up from the valley heralding the coming winter. The moon sheds its cold lemon tints, but the blood-red of an invisible sun illuminates the sky and fires the Clumps to a new life. The contrast of delicate, essentially pastel, colours and troubled brush strokes emphasizes the mood of uncertainty of the future.

Abstract
in Black, White, Maroon and Ochre
1957
122.2 × 122.2cm
Third prize in the John Moores Liverpool Exhibition I, 1957
and presented by John Moores

Victor Pasmore
Born 1908

The art of Victor Pasmore has always expressed the effects of light and space found in nature. In the 1930s and 1940s he painted figurative pictures of people and landscapes, transcribing the world as perceived by the senses onto the two dimensions of the canvas. The logical conclusion of these interests was to move into the third dimension, so as to deal with real space and with the changing effects of actual light on the projecting structure. Pasmore saw himself as moving from 'the idea of imitating the experience of beauty . . . to that of creating and constructing it.' In his view, 'There cannot be one law for nature and another for art,' since both operate in the same way when they are experienced by the viewer.

This painted wooden construction provides constantly changing patterns of shadow and sensations of space according to the fall of light and the viewer's position. Studied directly from the front, the Abstract functions like an ordinary painting, that is to say as a combination of flat geometrical shapes on the surface. Viewed from an angle, however, it is evident that while some forms are painted directly onto the background, others project at a right angle from the surface. The first impression is one of extreme severity: the forms are lined up in two rows on either side of the vertical axis, and only four colours are used, the chief of which is a 'non-colour,' white. Closer examination reveals the subtle asymmetries and the complex displacement of the rectangular forms from the rigid underlying structure. Similarly, a sparing use of colour creates conflicting sensations: the white forms, for example, seem both to float above the surface and to declare their identity as part of an uninterrupted solid form. The black, maroon and ochre bring the eye back to the surface but also suggest optical recession into or through the surface.

No single experience is the correct one. The object is perceived differently according to the light falling on it and according to its position in relation to the viewer and to the space of the room in which it hangs. It is in this sense that Constructivist artists such as Pasmore think of their work in relation to architecture. Their paintings are not escapes from reality into illusion but a means of intensifying in as pure a form as possible the operation of the viewer's senses.

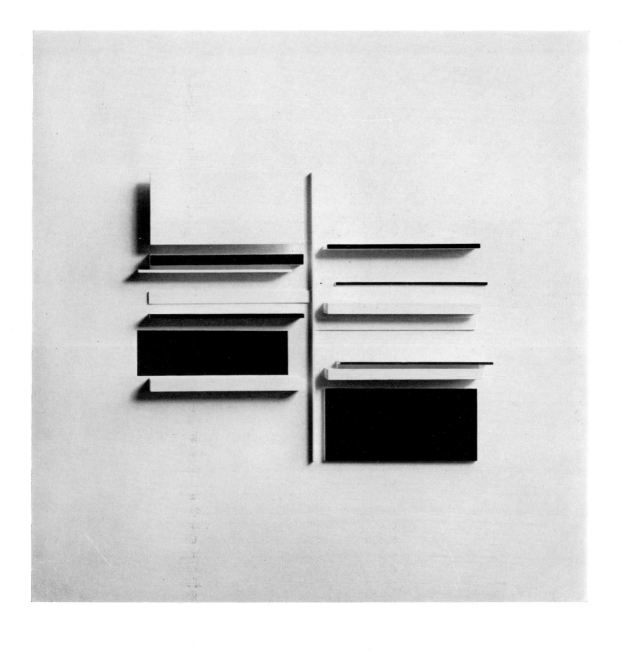

Peter Getting Out of Nick's Pool

213.4×213.4cm

First prize in the John Moores Liverpool Exhibition VI, 1967
and presented by John Moores, 1968

David Hockney

Born 1937

Photographs have been used as aids to painting for more than one hundred years. For Hockney the photo is not just a tool: it is an integral part of the theme of his work, since he wishes the viewer to know that images produced by a camera have been used in the making of the picture. The square format and white border of the painting immediately call to mind the Polaroid prints which Hockney referred to for both the figure and architecture. In mimicking an enlarged snapshot, the canvas proclaims its identity as an object which is real in its own right. The viewer knows that a photograph is flat, so the artist can imply spatial depth while maintaining the literal reality of the image as paint on a flat surface.

Hockney's painting is not a simple transcription of a single photograph. His friend Peter was leaning against a car, not pulling himself out of a swimming pool, when Hockney snapped the shutter. The reflections on the window were not set down from direct observation outdoors; the regular diagonal lines are copied from the type of illustrations found in mail-order catalogues, where they function as a kind of visual shorthand signifying light on a hard reflective surface. The interlaced curving lines in the pool are not exactly as Hockney would have perceived the patterns on the tiled floor through moving water; they are abstracted signs of flowing movement which are knowingly borrowed from the sinuous forms of art nouveau decoration. What might have appeared at first sight as a straightforward naturalistic description thus emerges as a composite view. Each element – carefully studied and (in the best sense) highly contrived – has passed through a filtering process of simplification and stylization. Through the combination of references, Hockney insists on the role of long-established pictorial devices allied to direct observation in the formulation of the painted image.

On a more personal level, this painting is a kind of snapshot souvenir of America as seen through Hockney's eyes. It is one of a series of pictures based on Hollywood swimming pools, most of which were painted while Hockney was teaching at the University of California at Los Angeles in 1966. Peter is Peter Schlesinger, a friend of his there; Nick Wilder, an art gallery owner, had the pool. Concentrating on the most exaggerated characteristics of California life – the strong light of perpetual summer, the lush vegetation carefully confined to tight suburban requirements, and the huge picture windows which make the outdoors a feature of the typical home – Hockney presents us with a convincing image of the American West Coast as a land of wish-fulfillment.

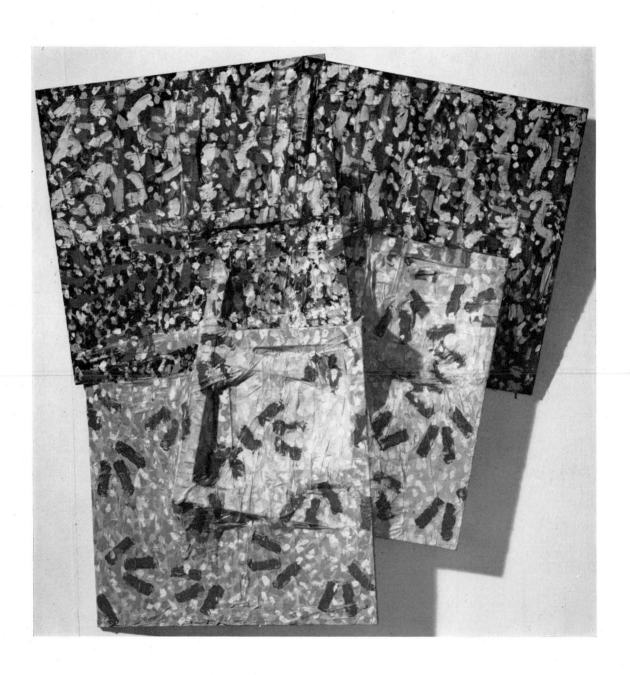

Head of a Young Girl No.1

1974
180.5 × 165 × 28cm
Purchased with the aid of the Calouste Gulbenkian Foundation's
Regional Purchase Scheme, 1978

Stephen Buckley
Born 1944

A primary concern of modern artists has been to reveal the processes which the artist has used to make his work. One way of doing this is to emphasize that the painting is a physical object. This painting by Stephen Buckley consists of four separate stretchers which have been woven together with interlaced bandages of canvas. The structure juts out aggressively from the wall, allowing the viewer a useful glimpse of the back of the picture to see how the bandages of canvas have been tied over the stretcher bars. Along the edges one can see the undercoat of paint, making one aware of the artist's actions in adding the successive layers of colour in simple decorative patterns. This concern for surface has a unifying effect, yet each of the four square stretchers maintains its individual identity through a particular combination of colours and decorative patterns.

This is one of a series of *Heads of Young Girls* which the artist titled in homage to the Cubist movement of the early part of this century. It is not intended as a representation of a young woman's features but rather as an analysis of a particular historical mode of painting. The facetting and interpenetration of planes has strong parallels with the treatment of the human head in Cubist paintings, in which multiple viewpoints were used to suggest simultaneous images of the front, side and back of the sitter. Buckley makes these suggestions explicit, since the viewer is allowed to see the painting from every angle, and the imaginary movement of the spectator now gives way to literal motion. In making the viewer walk around his painting to gain a full knowledge of its construction, Buckley acknowledges that the creative act is a two-part process, a collaboration between the artist and spectator.

Still Life – Autumn Fashion
1978
61 × 76.2cm

Purchased with the aid of the Calouste Gulbenkian Foundation's
Regional Purchase Scheme and a Grant-in aid
from the Victoria and Albert Museum
1979

Patrick Caulfield
Born 1936

Caulfield has long been interested in the potential of the cliche, and particularly in the relation of debased popular taste to the profound aesthetic experience encountered in the great art of the past. Fundamental to this concern is the conviction that decorative values are a primary source of pleasure in that all decoration involves a search for beauty through order. In this painting, for instance, Caulfield has devised a wallpaper pattern which in its colour scheme and design is intentionally grating and old-fashioned. Slowly, however, one begins to appreciate the logic and simplicity of this formal arrangement of basic geometric shapes, and even the rather odd green and brown colour scheme becomes acceptable when viewed in terms of the colours of autumn.

Implicit in the long history of the still life theme is the notion of arranging objects as a metaphor for composing forms in a painting. Caulfield is particularly keen to make the viewer aware of this process of making a picture, and he does so above all through a self-conscious manipulation of style, paralleling the deliberate spatial distortions and inconsistencies which likewise insist on the power of the artist to direct our attention. The artist poses a simple but crucial question: How does a representational picture relate to the perceived reality which it depicts? In making many references to art itself – to the traditional still life theme, to Cubist devices, and to Photo-Realism in the highly-detailed passages – Caulfield recognizes that prior knowledge inevitably affects the way in which we see things. The painter 'pictures' objects not as they are, but rather according to conventions established by artists over a period of time.

There are numerous references in Caulfield's painting to the Cubist delight in games of illusion and reality. The fundamental game in a representational picture, of course, involves the viewer as a willing accomplice who accepts the artist's fabrications in paint as a credible sign for an actual scene. This is made clear by making one material pose as another, as in the imitation wood grain of the pepper mill, since it makes one conscious that all representational images involve a transference from three-dimensional into two-dimensional form and from various materials into paint.

The bringing together of disparate modes relates to the Cubist technique of collage, in which a single picture is constructed from a number of segments of clearly different origin. Radically different techniques are juxtaposed as a means of drawing attention to their separate qualities. Some of the oysters, for instance, are defined by means of a thick black outline and a schematic rendering of the internal form; would these be immediately identifiable as oysters if it were not for the photographic precision of the remaining two oysters on the plate? We end up asking ourselves how much detail, what degree of imitation of surface appearances is necessary for recognition. We are thus made conscious of the wide choice facing an artist in selecting a style, and we are made to understand that any style is only a shorthand or coded language through which the artist communicates to the spectator.

R. P. Bonington:
**Sea Piece
(Ships in a Calm)**
Sudley Art Gallery

William Mulready:
A Dog of Two Minds
Sudley Art Gallery

Edwin Landseer:
Deer Stalking
Sudley Art Gallery

Sudley, an early nineteenth century house and grounds, together with its picture collection was bequeathed to the City of Liverpool by Miss Emma Holt in 1944. The collection was built up by her father, George Holt (1825–1896), a member of a notable shipping family. It reflects the taste of the period, being composed of early nineteenth century landscapes, works by the Pre-Raphaelites, the academic classicists and the late eighteenth century portraitists, against a background of genre paintings.

The collection includes the portrait of *Viscountess Folkestone*, painted by Gainsborough about 1776. The treatment is of great delicacy, with a misty colour scheme of greys and greens, and contrasts of airy gauzes, sheeny silks and soft grey hair, yet the old lady's force of character makes this one of the most powerful of Gainsborough's portraits.

Besides this, there is an outstanding group of late Turners, including *Rosenau* (illustrated in colour on p.14), a work highly praised by Ruskin, and two brilliant small landscapes by Bonington and Corot.

Sudley Art Gallery is in Mossley Hill, off Rose Lane, by Mossley Hill Church.

Bus services:
82 Pier Head to Speke. Stops at Aigburth Vale. Frequency 10 mins. 25/85 Walton to Garston. Stops at Aigburth Vale. Frequency 10 mins. 61 Seaforth to Aigburth. Stops at Aigburth Vale. Frequency 10 mins. 20/20A/21 Fazakerley to Aigburth Vale. Frequency 10 mins. 80 Pier Head to Speke. Stops at Templemore Avenue. Frequency 10 mins.

Train service:
To Mossley Hill Station from Lime Street, Liverpool to Crewe service and Liverpool to Warrington service.
Trains from Central Station Liverpool to Garston service to Aigburth Station.

Thomas Gainsborough:
Viscountess Folkestone
Sudley Art Gallery

Joshua Reynolds:
Elizabeth Gunning, Duchess of Hamilton and Argyll
Lady Lever Art Gallery

The Lady Lever Art Gallery
Port Sunlight

The Lady Lever Art Gallery is in the centre of Port Sunlight Village, Wirral, Cheshire.

Bus services:
39/41 from Birkenhead Woodside to Port Sunlight. Stops at New Chester Road Secondary School. Number 10 also from Birkenhead Woodside. Stops at Bebington Station.

Train service:
The Rock Ferry train from any Loop Line station. Change at Rock Ferry for the Port Sunlight train and then get off at Bebington station for the Gallery.

The outstanding collection formed by the 1st Viscount Leverhulme and the Gallery he built in memory of his wife in the centre of his model village of Port Sunlight, was opened in 1922. In 1978 its management was transferred by its Trustees to the care of Merseyside County Council. The collection of fine and decorative art, with particular emphasis on English achievements of the eighteenth century, complements and enhances the picture collections of the Walker Art Gallery and Sudley.

Lord Leverhulme (1851–1925) vividly reflected the taste of his day while concentrating on a limited number of carefully chosen fields with a remarkable eye for quality. The core of the collection at Port Sunlight (which is only a part of his immense collecting activities) is the superb eighteenth century English furniture. With this are paintings of the same period, Wedgwood pottery, Chinese porcelain, particularly blue and white of the K'ang Hsi period, prestigious English paintings of his own day, Masonic items, and, exceptional to the concentration on English art, a group of Napoleonic furniture and relics.

The paintings range from the famous portrait of *Elizabeth Gunning, Duchess of Hamilton and Argyll* by Reynolds, to Lord Leighton's *Garden of the Hesperides* and Turner's beautiful water-colour of *Hafod*. The furniture illustrates the finest craftsmanship with particular emphasis on commodes, chairs and tables of the eighteenth century in all their variety of woods and forms of decoration. The Wedgwood pottery in particular, illustrates the harmonious blending of mass production with design of the highest quality.

It is the combination of the period flavour of the great late Victorian and Edwardian collector with outstanding quality which makes the collection so exceptional.

William Holman Hunt:
The Scapegoat
Lady Lever Art Gallery

Satinwood commode
c. 1770
Lady Lever Art Gallery

Frederick Leighton:
The Garden of the Hesperides
Lady Lever Art Gallery

ISBN 0 901534 71 4

Type set in Monotype Plantin
and printed in Great Britain by
Lund Humphries,
London and Bradford